W9-AYD-179

ARE YOU KIDDING, GOD?

ME, a Prudent Woman?

DISCOVERING HIDDEN TREASURES IN UNEXPECTED PLACES

BY MELISSA JANSEN

WARNER PRESS

ANDERSON, INDIANA

All scripture quotations in this publication are from The Holy Bible, New International Version. Copyright © 1973, 1978, 1984 International Bible Society. Used by permission of Zondervan Bible Publishers.

Copyright © 1998 by Warner Press, Inc
ISBN 0-87162-815-5

All Rights Reserved
Printed in the United States of America
Warner Press, Inc

David C. Shultz, Editor in Chief
C. Richard Craghead, Editor
Cover and Layout by
Curtis D. Corzine and Virginia L. Wachenschwanz
Illustrations by Doug Hall
Photo by Linda Riedel Shively

CONTENTS

Foreword

Introduction

DEDICATION

I would like to dedicate this book to many people. Since I am not likely to ever win an Oscar I will make my thank-yous now.

Lord: Thank you for challenging us to live a prudent lifestyle. Please continue to bless this project in your own mysterious ways.

Paul: How did I get such an awesome man? Thank you for your help and support in the writing of this book. You are such a prudent guy. I love you.

Adam, Ryan, and Madison: You are my treasures. Even though you hardly know I wrote a book, I just can't waste a chance to tell you how much I love you. Save up your allowance and buy Mommy's book.

Ken and Judy Mishler: Dad and Mom, you were the first to tell me to write this book and you were the most supportive people to me through this whole process. I love you more than I could ever say. Thank you.

Karen Rhodes: My own personal "God-appointed" advocate. I praise the Lord for you.

And last I would like to thank the Academy for this great honor. Thank you.

FOREWORD

I have a real heart for moms and dads. Parents these days struggle so hard to make sense of the madcap race between careers, home, school, baby-sitters, and church. It's tough in the 90s to balance all the demands placed upon us. Depression and stress are running rampant. It has been my mission to help people see how a sense of humor and the grace of God can make life not only bearable, but some times even enjoyable.

When I ran across Missy's book I said to myself, "This book is GREAT! Here's a survivor! This young woman understands how to get by, how to laugh, and how to deal with disappointments. Missy knows how to appreciate but also how to persevere."

Melissa's book is a real encourager to moms who struggle with everyday problems and need a real injection of joy into their routine. Missy captures the reader's heart. Before long we feel a part of the encouragement she projects into her materials.

Is your budget lower than low? Not a problem! Entertain your kids with a popcorn popper and a sheet in the middle of the living room. Do you only have one or two outfits left in your wardrobe that fit, and those make you look like the jolly green giant and Barney? Read how Missy deals with those issues, too. Do you grit your teeth when the neighbor shops off the rack marked "new arrivals" while you shop from "clearance" racks or rummage sales? Missy's been there and doesn't mind talking about it.

Missy's added questions at the end of each chapter. For example,

- Do you consider yourself most in need spiritually, emotionally, or financially? Why?
- When is the last time you sat down, really looked into the eyes of your child and giggled?
- What drives you to the edge of your emotional cliff faster than anything else?

A women's Bible study or Sunday school group will learn a lot about themselves and the Bible by working through these issues.

I commend this book to you and pray you will hear God's laughter and see His smile through its pages.

Barbara Johnson
Director of Spatula Ministries
Popular author of many books, including
Stick a Geranium in Your Hat and Be Happy
Living Somewhere Between Estrogen and Death

Introduction

How many times, fellow bargain hunter, has this happened to you? You see a magazine in a check-out lane that says, "50 cheap ways to fix up your house!" With excitement you grab the magazine and pay for it out of your carefully budgeted grocery money, thinking it's okay because in the long run this magazine is going to save you oodles of money. You drive home, put the kids to bed, run to your favorite chair and open up your beloved new "bargain book." To your dismay, however, you see that one of the "cheap ways" happens to be buying an antique couch for $900 rather than the $1,200 one they were going to buy in the first place. You now get up and place this magazine with the stack of others whose combined prices add up to the $900 you could have used to buy the couch.

I stopped buying magazines like that. I found that their ideas were on a completely different level than I was. So if you are cheap like me—whether by choice or necessity—maybe my tips will be a little more in your price range.

Proverbs 19:14 says, "Houses and wealth are inherited from parents, but a prudent wife is from the Lord." Prudent, now there's a word that creates excitement! I ask you, "Who wants to be a prudent woman?" A tight-lipped woman with a high collar and her hair up in a bun is the mental picture I have always had of a prudent woman. In fact, in the past I have labeled such women as "old prudes." That's why this proverb hit me so hard. Does

God desire me to be boring and uptight? I ran to my dictionary, and here's what I read: "Prudent-*adj.* Exercising sound judgment in practical matters." Hey, I like that! I want to exercise sound judgment.

How about you? If you were asked to close your eyes and imagine a woman who exercised sound judgment in every situation and area in her life, what would she look like to you? If you gazed at her calendar, what would her schedule look like? If you asked her friends about her, what would they say? What would her children say about her? How would she spend her "free time"? If you could listen to her conversations, what would she be saying? Most importantly, if you were somehow able to see right into the depths of her soul, what would it show she values and invests herself in the most? Prudence is a discipline that can affect every area, attitude, and relationship in your life.

When I think of a woman who might model excellence in being prudent, I think of the famous woman the Bible tells us about in the last chapter in Proverbs (I even find her a touch annoying because of her accomplishments). She is called a wife of noble character and her example is one tough act to follow. Listen to just a few of the amazing roles and disciplines this woman possesses.

First of all, in verse 15 she already is a catch for any man because she gets up before the sun and cooks, not only for the family, but also for the workers. I drag myself out of bed at about 6:00 A.M. to stick a Pop-Tart in the toaster and pour a glass of Kool-Aid for my husband as he heads off for work every morning. I realize that I might have missed the mark on this first target.

Verse 16 says, "She considers a field and buys it; out of her earnings she plants a vineyard." This wonderful lady buys property and farms it. I, on the other extreme, buy geraniums and kill them. (Did you know you have to water those things?)

A few verses later the Bible shows what a generous spirit this "noble wife" displays. She opens her arms to the poor and extends her hands to the needy.

Proverbs goes on to describe this woman as laughing at the days to come simply because she is prepared for them. Winter does not scare her; she has already sewn coats for the family. Her husband is respected because of her. Her children think she's fabulous, and rightly so. When she speaks, verse 26 says she does it with wisdom. This passage comes to a close in verse 30 with a rather famous verse: "Charm is deceptive, and beauty is fleeting; but a woman who fears the Lord is to be praised."

When I see all the areas in which this woman displays prudent living, I realize I have two choices. The first is to cut Proverbs 31 out of my husband's Bible so he doesn't get any ideas. The second is to be challenged enough to change. This is what I believe this chapter was meant to do. I want to please God with the things I buy. I want to please God with how willing I am to give. I want to please God in how I serve my family and community. All these choices relate to the huge discipline of being prudent. In the chapters of this book I hope you also will be challenged to change.

While writing this book, I have asked myself several times, "Missy, you sweet thing, why are you so cheap?" I can honestly say that for as long as I can remember I have tried to make the most of a buck. I love to get a great bargain! However, I have also realized that money always burns a hole in my pocket. When I do have money, I want to spend it—now.

My brother Doug has always been different from me in that he saves things. Every Christmas morning Chris (my oldest brother), Doug, and I would go to our stockings and empty out every last item. Any fruit was immediately put in the kitchen where somebody besides us could eat it. After that we each would take a shoe box and put all our candy in it. Threats would spew out of my brothers' mouths, warning me of terrible plagues and destruction that would come my way if I ever ventured into their boxes. Well, I always rung in the New Year with an empty shoe box and a chin covered with chocolate. Chris seemed to empty his box at a normal pace. Doug, on the other hand, still would be nibbling on a Christmas Kit-Kat bar the following Halloween.

Doug not only saved his Christmas candy, he saved other things, like his old shoes. His closet floor was covered with tennis shoes of all colors and styles that he couldn't bear to get rid of. I also remember Doug as always having money. He didn't go out and blow it as I did. Then again, unlike him, I had to buy more candy. Even now as an adult Doug and his wife, Holly, are very disciplined with their money. They have a wonderful budget that they stick to faithfully. Doug is just good at stuff like that. If he'd only get rid of some of his old tennis shoes, he'd be a really great guy.

When it comes to being prudent, Doug's personality gives him an advantage over me. Being careful with money and possessions comes naturally to him. I don't know from which ancestor he inherited that trait, but I don't think poor Chris and I got those genes. We have to work harder at it, but that's okay because we're better looking. (Only kidding, Dougie!)

As you continue through this book, some of the areas I discuss you might already have under control simply because of the character God gave you. You might have to examine other areas thoughtfully and make changes. I'll be the first to admit I'm not a prudent woman yet, at least not in every area; however, God has taught me a great deal, and he isn't done with me. I just might be an old prude yet! I hope you will join me on my journey.

· *Chapter 1* ·

COMMITTED
TO
CONTENTMENT

> Making a case for prudence: "If ... you are wanting to update what you have or perhaps you feel you need to make a change, then I want to encourage you to do so. [But] I want to show you an alternative to 'heavy' spending."

You know not having money stinks! I'm serious. Not having money rains on my parade more than anything else. Oh, how many times I would like to hop on a plane and go to Florida for a week to relax with my family. Drip, drop. Or go to a real salon to cut and color my hair instead of to my own bathroom. Drip, drop. Or even be free to have friends over for a nice dinner anytime we wanted. Drip, drop. These things are not totally selfish desires. These are just everyday, ordinary things. Drip, drop, drip, drop. It's raining again, all over my parade of wants! If only Paul could get a big raise, then we could....

I'm uncomfortably aware that the writer of Ecclesiastes had me in mind when he wrote:

> Whoever loves money never has money enough;
> whoever loves wealth is never satisfied
> with his income.
> This too is meaningless.
> —Ecclesiastes 5:10

The prudent woman of Proverbs 31 seems to have gained control of this thirst for acquiring things. I can't help but notice that her discipline did not turn her into a cynic, like the Ecclesiastes author, nor did it keep her from being a productive and positive-thinking woman. I hope someday to have a measure of her contentment.

No matter how much I think the lack of money stinks, I have to confess to you that I fight with having a deep love for the "abundance of money." I love to think of the things I could do with money. I would like to have a whole bunch of it and buy a big white farmhouse with lots of character. Then I'd buy old antiques and fill up my big white farmhouse with lots of character. I want to pass by rooms in my house and occasionally think, "Oh, I forgot about that one."

I'd reach into my heavy purse and pay someone to clean my big white farmhouse with lots of character. I'd buy my kids beautiful clothes at the mall from racks marked "New Arrivals" instead of "Clearance." I'd buy toys that need batteries without even considering how much money it would take to replace the old batteries. I'd order clothes for myself from catalogs, and I'd go to one of those weight-loss spas where all I'd have to do is lie on a machine that would exercise for me. I'd load all my stuff in my hot little red sports car (with room for a couple of car seats, of course) and drive back to my big white farmhouse with lots of character. My husband would adore me, and it would be worth his while to do so. My kids would be the envy of all the middle class kids from down the street because of their dirt bikes and radio-controlled model cars.

Oh, doesn't that sound delicious? Actually, that is a wild exaggeration of what I would do with an abundance of money, but some of it rings true (especially the big white farmhouse with lots of character). My point is, I fear that no matter how much money Paul and I bring in, I would always find a way to spend it on bigger and better things, things we really don't need. Is that what the Lord would have me do? Is that being prudent with what I have? What would the woman of Proverbs 31 think and do if she were in my place?

I gained some insight into my own character while reflecting upon a very common household incident. It was lunchtime for my four-year-old, Adam, and my two-year-old, Ryan. I made two peanut butter and jelly sandwiches. Adam said in his half-talking, half- singing tone, "I want that sandwich; it has more jelly." I poured the Kool-Aid. Again Adam chimed, "I want the cup with the blue lid; it has more Kool-Aid." I gave each of them a cookie. "I want that one; it's bigger and has more chocolate chips!" cried Adam. You know, that frustrates me. Why must he always want more? I find myself mentally rooting for Ryan to get the bigger cookie, the cup with more Kool-Aid. I can't help it. When Adam is never satisfied with what I give him, he takes away my joy of giving.

This annoying habit of Adam's hit me hard one day as I daydreamed, once again, of a bigger house. I was having my quiet time and praying about moving when it struck me. "I'm Adam. I'm never satisfied." I felt my soul cringe in embarrassment and shame as I wrote in my journal, "Please forgive me, Father! I am just a child. I act like the child who always wants the bigger cookie, the cup with more Kool-Aid. Forgive me and help me to turn from my selfishness and change."

To help cement the moment in my mind I looked up Hebrews 13:5 which says, "Keep your lives free from the love of money and be content with what you have, because God has said, 'Never will I leave you; never will I forsake you.' " You see, I, and probably we, need to get out of the "If only I had" mind set, and enter into the "I'm so thankful I have" zone. Let's be joyful in all God has given us, otherwise we may take away his joy of giving. Also, let's not ignore the ending of that wonderful verse we just read where God makes a promise. It was not a promise that he will keep giving us more. No, instead God graciously promises that whether we find ourselves living in plenty or in want, he will never leave us. That is of much more value than anything this temporary world can offer us.

The Apostle Paul grasped this concept with both hands. Listen to his words which are recorded in Philippians 4:11b–13:

> I have learned to be content whatever the circumstances. I know what it is to be in need, and I know what it is to have plenty. I have learned the secret of being content in any and every situation, whether well fed or hungry, whether living in plenty or in want. I can do everything through him who gives me strength.

I can't honestly say I have totally grasped the "content in everything" concept yet, but I'm trying. I know that's what God has called me to—called us to.

When I started to write this book, my goal was to develop a simple set of ideas about saving money by rummaging, decorating on a shoestring, and entertaining friends and children on a low budget; however, the more I wrote about being prudent the more the subject grew. I tried to keep the areas touched by prudency limited, but it was like trying to wrap a full length mink coat in a jewelry box. My small vision of being prudent in my life went from limited to all-encompassing. You see, God did not call us to be prudent in a couple of neat little areas in our lives. He has called us, as Christians, to exercise sound judgment in all areas of our lives. Our budget, time, children, prayer life, activities, even decorating—all are touched by this discipline.

As you continue through this book I hope you don't find me pushing you to buy things, whether at rummage sales or stores, that you do not need. I don't want to push you to redecorate when you are quite happy with the way things are. That is not my intent. If, however, you are wanting to update what you have or perhaps feel you need to make a change, then I want to encourage you to do so. If you need to make some purchases, I want to show you an alternative to "heavy" spending. Now that you know my intentions are the purest of pure, I hope you find some bits of knowledge (I mean little bitty bits) in this book.

By wisdom a house is built, and through understanding it is established; through knowledge its
rooms are filled with rare and beautiful treasures.
                                    —Proverbs 24:3–4

Journal

ON THE SURFACE ...

1. What if money were not an issue? Describe what kind of house you would have. Where would it be? How big? How would you decorate it?

_____

_____

_____

_____

_____

_____

2. Do you see yourself as a *spender* or a *saver?* Are you satisfied with what you are?

_____

_____

_____

_____

_____

3. Who do you know handles their money with prudent wisdom? What do they do differently than you do?

_____

_____

_____

_____

_____

UNDER THE SKIN ...

Reread Philippians 4:11–14.

1. Do you consider yourself most in need spiritually, emotionally, or financially? Why?

_____

_____

_____

_____

_____

_____

2. In what area do you have plenty? What makes it plenty?

_____

_____

_____

_____

_____

_____

3. Do you experience the peace that comes from knowing the secret of contentment?

_____

_____

_____

_____

_____

_____

NOW WHAT ...?

1. Take a piece of paper and write the days of the week down the left side, skipping a few lines in between each day. Put the paper in a place where you have to see it often. Every day write out a thank-you to God for something for which you are truly grateful and have never thanked him before. Example: When you are cleaning up after dinner thank the Lord for your dishwasher that saves you time. Or, when you get out of bed tomorrow thank the Lord for water with which to shower. You get the idea. By thanking God for the little things, I've become truly grateful for all of his blessings to us.

SOMETHING TO PASS ON ...

Today, ask your child, "What item that you own would be the last one you would give up? Why?" Together, thank the Lord for that item.

Journal

· Chapter 2 ·

THE ART OF RUMMAGING

> "I am trying to learn that being a prudent shopper isn't always finding things at cheap prices, but also knowing when I actually need to stop looking all together."

It's Saturday morning. I find a rummage sale with a garage so full of toys and clothes that the merchandise spills out onto the yard. My heart beats wildly as I hear the lady in charge say, "Oh, I don't care how much money I make, I just want to get rid of it all!" Just as I give her $1.50 for the entire lot, I wake up in a cold sweat. It's only 3:00 A.M., and I have five more hours before the announced rummage sale hour.

I was going to start this book with a chapter on rummage sales. In fact, you will find a "rummage" theme carried throughout. I probably owe over half of everything in my house to rummages. Whether it be knickknacks, furniture, clothes, or toys, most are due to prudent shopping in hundreds of different garages.

My love affair with rummaging started early, since my mom took me with her almost every week. Every once in a while I would venture out on my own. Let me share with you one of my early memories of such an outing.

My friend and I were walking home from our elementary school when we passed a house with a driveway filled with rummage. We excitedly started going through the many tall barrels of toys. I remember looking up at the adults and smiling, thinking they must be impressed with how well we rummaged for such young girls. They just sat there with bewildered looks on their faces. I remember reaching way down into one of the barrels, pulling out a Fisher Price dollhouse and asking, "How much do you want for this house?" The answer I received still makes my cheeks blush.

One of the ladies who had been watching us so closely said, "We aren't having a rummage sale. We're just cleaning out our garage!" Well, I could have died. My friend and I ran away, unable to get anything to come out of our mouths except an occasional giggle. The family did have a rummage sale the following weekend, but I was too embarrassed to go.

As awful as that experience was, it didn't curtail the enjoyment I get out of rummaging. Nearly every Saturday, I take $5.00 (unless I have been saving up for something special), the rummage section in the newspaper, and I'm off for an exciting morning of adventure. Joining me in this quest is usually my sweet friend Karen. I swing by to pick her up and off we go from garage to garage shopping for new and old items that tickle our fancies.

What can I find for such a small financial investment? Oh, let's see. One Saturday I got a wonderful Fisher Price toy that changes into many different instruments (which has already provided hours of entertainment for the whole family, not to mention a headache for Mom!), two hardboard puzzles, a vase for my summer lilacs, and a hardback book, all for a total of ninety cents. How about that? Am I in your price range? This is not a strange occurrence; it happens almost weekly. All it takes is a little patience, hunting, and imagination. After a while you get a feeling for the range of prices generally posted for similar items. If you find an item you'd like to buy, it never hurts to ask politely if the owner would accept less. The instrument I bought was marked $1.00, but I got it for $.50. Little price reductions really add up at the end of the day.

I like to start off my rummage sale day with the newspaper. In my paper all the sales are divided into the north, south, east, and west quadrants of my town. This makes it very convenient for me since a sense of direction is not my strong point. As I read through the paper I like to mark the sales in the order of my interest and cross out the sales I am not interested in. For instance, I usually avoid sales that have been going on for a couple days.

I have three children, about two years apart from each other: Adam Paul, Ryan Solomon, and Madison Joanna, the youngest. So for me and my friend Karen a sale advertising toys or children's clothes would be one we would head for first. We also have decided that if a neighborhood is having a rummage sale which draws a huge crowd, we have good luck by heading to other sales first. We avoid the crowds, and we get to see what the other less picked-over sales are offering. Do you think I take rummaging a little too seriously? Wait, I'm not done yet.

A new thing Karen and I have tried to put together recently is a little book to help us remember where roads are. Many times we feel we waste time trying to remember where Elm Street is. We know we've been there before, but was it by the Dairy Queen or Kmart? So I bought a little address book, and now every time we find a street with which we are not familiar, we list it in our book.

For example, if we finally find "Oak Drive," we can write it down under "O" and give basic directions written in our own words, "Go to George's cleaners and turn toward that big blue house with the cool light out front. Oak Drive is two roads down." Next time there is a sale there we can look up the street and find it right away. Consequently, we won't miss any fabulous items that would have been sold to somebody else while we were saying, "I know we've been there before...." Karen also brings her map of our town (my birthday present to her) to help us find our way. Are you worried about us? Really we are quite normal people; we just love our rummages!

Another thing that might seem a tad strange about us is our firm belief that we should delay our visits to sales in a ritzy neighborhood until after we have gone to the middle to lower income areas. "Why?" you ask. The reason is, people who pay more for their things expect higher prices. In fact, sometimes I leave a big beautiful home with a huge carpeted garage just laughing. It's amazing that even in rummaging you pay for the neighborhood. Now that doesn't mean you will never find a good deal at a nice home, because I have many times. I just want to encourage you not to be too influenced by the address.

You are now at the sale. You're surrounded by a mass of people whose goal must be to touch every item on the tables. It can get quite confusing sometimes. Let me give you some tips to remember as you move among the other browsers.

CLOTHES

Look everything over well. It amazes me how people think that even though that old white shirt has oil stains all over it, it should be worth a buck because it has a "Levi" tag on the shirt pocket. If something has a stain and you still want it, go to the person in charge and nicely say, "Hey, I notice this has a stain. Would you take a quarter?" or whatever price pleases your pocketbook. I just can't stress enough not to overpay for things.

On the other hand, I tend to be so cheap that I miss out on some very nice outfits. I need to remember that if I find an outfit that is in great shape and something I could really put to use, it's okay to pay a little more. Not long ago I came home with only two outfits to show for my $5.00, both for my little Ryan. But you know, I have already gotten my money's worth out of them, and he looks wonderful! I'd say those outfits were a prudent investment.

Also, while shopping for clothes, remember to think about the future. If you find a handsome sweater for a good price, don't let the sweat on your forehead stop you from buying it for your son to wear this winter. Or if you find a beautiful dress that is a size 7, but your daughter now wears a size 6, perhaps you should buy it and save it for next year. I think that's exercising sound judgment in a practical matter. Unless, of course, your daughter already has a closet full of clothes for next year. If that's the case, let it hang there!

FURNITURE

I had the "newlywed table" for four years. You know the one—the fake brass legs and glass top. It has those nice places where the glass and wood connect and where all the crumbs from dinner collect. Let's not forget the chairs. My chairs swayed so much I almost lost my supper as soon as I ate it, due to motion sickness. If you have one of these tables, I don't mean to poke fun at yours, but mine was old and really needed to retire. So when Paul and I bought our first home, I was ready for a new table. I began to pray that the Lord would lead me to one I could afford. Well, it wasn't too long until I found four lonely black chairs. They had the cutest style and were only $5.00 for all four of them. I stored them in the garage until I could find a table for them to accompany.

A few weeks later I went to another rummage sale. Adam and I picked out some little items, and just as I turned to go I noticed an old table that was being used to set things on for the sale. I asked if it was for sale. The lady said, "Let me go ask my mother." She came back and said, "Well, my mom wasn't planning on selling it, but for the right price she said she would." I remember thinking, "Well, I have twenty collars in my purse that I have been saving. Should I say twenty? No, I don't want to embarrass the mother. She probably wants a lot more for it than that."

My thinking was interrupted as the lady said, "My mom said she would be happy if she could get $7.50 for it." Trying not to act quite as ecstatic as I felt at that moment, I said, "Well, huh. Let me see how much I have." For one evil moment I almost said, "Would you take $5.00?" But instead I said, "I'll take it!"

We brought it home and started working on it immediately.

First, my patient husband sanded and sanded. It was in pretty good shape, but it did have a rough stain and small scratches that needed to be sanded off. After he got it smooth, I started my specialty: strange new ideas. At that time "marbleizing" things was the new trend. I bought a kit that showed me how to do it step by step. It cost me about $10.00 so I was really praying it would turn out well.

The first thing I had to do was paint the top of my table black. Next, I sponged on different colors of green and followed up with light feather painting of white. I painted the legs of my table white and covered the whole table with a good quality polyurethane. Polyurethane is a "must" with a project like this. It adds durability and a much richer look. After the table was finished, I marbleized my chairs to match. I want to tell you, I loved it! I mean I LOVED it! I even kept my kitchen clean so my table would be noticed more. That didn't last long, but it was a nice little period in my life.

I might add you can marbleize in any color and the expense is low. I bought my table, four chairs, and paint all for under $30.00. Can you stand it!

I'm not trying to sound like, "Hey, look at me. Aren't I amazing!" No, I'm telling you this because if I can do it, I know you can, too. If you have the interest in doing such a project, the possibilities are endless. You can pick up an old table and chairs that don't even match each other and paint them to look like they do. Go crazy; be original. Paint checkerboards. Cut out wallpaper flowers and stick them on. Stencil around the edges. Gracious, there are so many things to spice up something dull. The best reward from doing this is just that, you did it! People would see my new table and pay us nice compliments on how pretty it looks. Of course, my kitchen was clean. They might have been in shock.

TOYS

Don't let a little dirt fool you. I am always glad to find a toy that needs a little tender loving care. Do you know why? Because I can buy it cheaper. SOS cleans rusty chrome to a shiny reflection. Plain old soap and water can do miracles, too! I'm not saying to buy something that smells like my husband's jogging shorts, but don't miss out on a great deal just because of a little work.

I hate to sound monotonous, but once again remember not to pay too much. This is a hard call to make for other people, but as for me, I am not willing to pay a lot. I have seen some of the little Fisher Price houses with the people and cars in truly wonderful condition go for $8.00 or so, and I say to myself, "$8.00! Don't they know this is a rummage sale!" That, to me, is too much to pay; however, others swoop it off the table thinking they have just found the sale of the century.

As I continue, you might find me cheap. That's fine, in fact, because I find myself cheap. There are times that I do pay more for a certain toy. One time I found a "Whirl Bird" bike by Little Tykes. I don't know if you have ever seen one, but I thought it was so cool and in great shape. The seller wanted $7.00. I asked for $5.00; but she stood firm. I thought about it and realized for a name brand as good and solid as Little Tykes, $7.00 really wasn't too bad a price. Maybe you don't watch your money as closely as I do, but remember that no matter what we have, we need to prudently use the resources with which the Lord has blessed us.

Most, and I do mean most, of the toys in my house are from rummage sales. For instance, I took an inventory of the toys lying on the floor in the room in which I was sitting one day, and there were sixteen. Thirteen of those toys came from rummage sales. Among them was a Little Tykes doctor's case, a stacking toy, and a wagon. None cost over $2.00. To look at them you would never know they were secondhand.

When I see a toy I like at a rummage sale, but it is priced too high, I hardly ever hesitate to ask the seller to take what I would be willing to give. You might be surprised at how eager the seller may be just to get rid of everything. Always ask with kindness and offer a specific amount. For instance, if you see a toy for $5.00 for which you would give $3.00, don't say, "Ma'am, would you take less for this?" More than likely she will either say, "Well, how much are you thinking?" or "No, I don't think so." People who have a busy sale going on don't want to have to think about a barter price. It almost seems easier to say no. Ask for a specific amount, and you will have a much better response.

I would like to end this toy-talk with a little story that is rather sad. It's sad because many times I have bought toys because they were cheap, not because I really had any use for them. I remember going to one sale and finding a bike. This bike was old, beaten up, and so sorry looking that I thought it was cute. It was the tiniest "big boy" bike I had ever seen. I gave the rummage owner fifty cents and off I went with my piece of yellow junk. I really thought that we could fix it up for our little Ryan. He would look so cute on it.

Do you know that in my garage still sits an ugly yellow bike that does nothing but gather dust. We probably never will fix it up; however, maybe the next person who came to that sale would have. I did not practice "prudent shopping" that time. That was called "stupid shopping." If that were the only time I had done that, it wouldn't be so bad, but I have bought many toys that were nothing more than a waste of my money. I am trying to learn that being a prudent shopper isn't always finding things at cheap prices, but also knowing when I actually need to stop looking all together. Sometimes that may mean I need to think of something else to do with my Saturday mornings. Maybe, I should work on that bike.

Journal

ON THE SURFACE ...

1. What article in your home do you consider the greatest bargain? _____

2. What is your favorite way to save money?

_____

_____

_____

UNDER THE SKIN ...

Philippians 4:19

"My God will meet all your needs according to his glorious riches in Christ Jesus."

1. Are you comfortable relying on God to meet your needs? What do you consider *relying on God?*

_____

_____

_____

2. Do you think God is more concerned with your comfort or your obedience? Why?

_____

_____

NOW WHAT ...?

1. I challenge you to get up this Saturday morning (if it is "Rummage Season") and look in your paper for any rummage sales. Now get dressed and go! If it is not the right time of year for garage sale mania, then try to find an auction to attend. If you can't find an auction just go to your neighbor's house and see if they will sell you something you need for a quarter.

SOMETHING TO PASS ON ...

Next time your child has a material need such as school clothes or a birthday party gift to purchase, let her or him decide how to spend the money. Even more important, make him or her live with the choices he or she makes. For example, if your child spends all his school clothes allowance on one cool pair of shoes instead of a pair of jeans and a couple of shirts, don't give in and hand him more money a couple of days into school when he sees the error of his ways. It's a great way for him to learn to budget more wisely next time. If it is a small child buying a friend's birthday gift, give her or him the $5.00 (or whatever) and let her or him try to find the best deal for her or his money. Chances are you'll find two regular occurrences: 1. Your child will pick out something you hate. 2. Your child will begin to understand that $5.00 doesn't give him or her a broad selection of gifts from which to choose. It's good for them to see how far a dollar actually goes.

· Chapter 3 ·

HOW TO BUILD A BETTER RUMMAGE SALE

> "It's awesome that the Lord can use us even in something as simple as a rummage sale."

I've got stuff. I mean, I've REALLY got stuff. If you look in my closets, you'll see clothes in a vast assortment of sizes and styles, many of which have not graced my body in years. I have shoes. My cousin Jackie gives me all her hand-me-down shoes, and I really love them, but I seldom wear them. We've got books, papers, toys, dishes, and furniture that gather dust in our dark closets, drawers, and attic. Poor little unwanted things; they need a good home!

It's time for a rummage sale! Yes, it's easy to go to a rummage sale, but do you know how to conduct a successful one? Let me give you some suggestions.

COLLECTING

Go from room to room in your house and gather all unwanted items. After you have done that, go through all your rooms again. This time get all your unneeded items. Do you really need three copies of that book? Will you ever be that size again? If so, will the clothes still be in style? (Boy, does that hit home with me!) Is it time to sell Rover's doggie bed now that Rover is buried in your flower bed? Yes! This is the day. Clean out those boxes under your bed that were marked "save." Hey, all this talk about cleaning has me exhausted, but let's continue.

PRICING

After everything is out in a big area where you can work, it's time to price. Buy some good big labels. The little ones will fall off too easily. First, write your initials somewhere on the tag. If you have someone else doing the sale with you, this makes it easier to divide up the money at the end. Also, write the size on the tag if you are selling clothes. Next, in big numbers put the price. Ahh, the price. This is the hardest part of the whole process. People, including myself, sometimes don't know what to charge.

Let's face a couple of facts right off the bat. One fact is that we want to get as much money for our things as we can. There isn't anything wrong with that, but that brings me to fact number two: our stuff probably isn't as spectacular as we may think. I have baby clothes from my boys that I have tried to sell for too much money. One was an outfit Ryan wore. Oh, he always looked so adorable in it! I put $3.00 or $4.00 on it. I couldn't wait to see the women wrestle over who had seen it first! It just sat there, however. I thought, "Don't these people know how cute my son looked in this?" Sadly, I had to realize that not only do these people not know these things, they don't even care. All they want is a good buy. That's all I want when I go rummaging (although I would have noticed the supreme quality and good looks of that outfit, I'm sure!). Let us remember this wise phrase as we price: Would I rather get a fair price for this outfit, or ask too much and lug it back into the house? You ask, "What, Missy, is a fair price?" All I can tell you is to guess. What would you pay for it? Then put it out and listen to what people are saying. If they look at your prices and laugh, that's not a good sign.

DISPLAYING

A good way to get as much as you can out of your items is to display them nicely. If you have dishes, make sure they are clean. Put them on a table instead of on the ground. If you are selling clothes, make sure they're clean. I wash all the clothes I sell. I even iron out the wrinkles. Anything you hang up will look nicer and therefore will probably sell for a little more. I get all the spots out of things that I can. For a sweat suit with a couple of spots I might ask $.50; however, if I get all the spots out and arrange it nicely, I might get $1.00. It's worth the effort at the end of the day.

If you are not willing to put an individual price on each outfit, then you need to have BIG signs that explain the prices well. Examples: Shirts—$.50; Pants—$.75. You probably won't do as well this way, and chances are people are still going to ask all day, "How much is this shirt? It doesn't have a price on it." You'll get sick of that early. Also, remember to be willing to take less than the price you're asking. You may not have to do this on everything, but keep an open mind.

MAKING SIGNS

Speaking of signs, make neat big ones for the street by your house. Put big arrows on them to lead the way. Include the date, time, and address. Your social security number and annual income also may be helpful. No, you don't have to put the last two, but do be specific and neat. After you are done, ask yourself if you would be able to read the sign going past it at about thirty-five miles per hour.

Balloons are a big help. If your house sits back off the road a distance, you might consider putting some balloons on your mailbox just to make sure nobody drives by, thus missing the sale of a lifetime.

One year, I made signs for the big streets that lead to my little street. Instead of being simple and writing "RUMMAGE" or "GARAGE SALE" in bold letters and adding an arrow or two, I felt like being a little fancy. I drew a lady saying what a great sale was just down the street. I made every sign a piece of artwork. They were awesome! I hung them up with pride. The whole day at my sale I heard little comments about how hard this street was to find. I couldn't believe it! Finally, I asked, "Didn't you see the signs I hung up, the ones with the pictures?" One lady said, "Oh, were those rummage sale signs? I didn't read them; they were too busy." All that work for nothing! So, I have found it's good to keep your signs simple.

ADVERTISING

Newspaper advertising is the wisest investment for your rummage sale. Make sure to include your address, time and date(s) of sale, and maybe even an attention getter such as: "Lots of baby items," "Large Woman's Clothes," or "Nice Furniture." These will draw in people who are looking for what you're offering.

STARTING

As far as what time to start, I like 8:00 A.M. That's the universal rummage hour. Of course, that usually means people expect to be let in by 7:30 A.M. If you don't want that to happen, put in your classified advertisement, "No early sales!" People will come early anyway but you may have held off some of the eager beavers. This is no joke.

One Saturday morning, I was sorting through the paper trying to plot out my prudent path of sales when I came upon an ad that said it would start at 5:00 A.M. I laughed at what I supposed was a person who decided she would put an end to those annoying "early bird" rummagers. I arrived at the sale at 7:30 A.M. and had to tell the man how much I enjoyed his ad. I couldn't believe it when he looked at me and rolled his eyes as he said, "It didn't do me any good. People started to show up at 4:30 this morning!" Can you believe it! I was shocked at the thought that there were people out there somewhere that might love to rummage even more than I.

There are many rude people in this world, while we're on this subject. Many of them are avid rummagers. Let me give you an example of tacky rummaging: People who show up at 6:00 A.M. for an 8:00 A.M. rummage and ask to see the goods. Often they come to your door armed with an excuse about having to work and can't make it at 8:00 A.M. I've heard of people who show up the night before the sale with an excuse about how they can't make it the next morning because they are having major surgery or something. I say if they can't make the sale during the sale, then tough toenails! Arriving early is not fair play for all of us who are proper, patient, and just plain good rummagers. I am always livid when I rush to a sale that advertised an item I am interested in, only to find out it has been sold to some stranger who came the night before. Oh, I'm ticked-off just thinking about it!

PROVIDING SECURITY

On the day of your sale, be ready on time. Sit at a table in a spot where people have to pass by you to go to their cars. Believe it or not, shoplifting can happen often. Now, you don't need to hire a security guard, but do take precautions to discourage pilferage. It's also a good idea to take your money inside every once in a while. I always do after my first $1,000 or so! (Would you believe $100 or so?)

Be friendly to everybody. Don't sit at your "throne" and look down your nose at the dirty little people going through your castoffs. (I have experienced that look before.) Talk and laugh with your visitors and show them Jesus through your attitude. Ephesians 4:2 says, "Be completely humble and gentle; be patient, bearing with one another in love." The Apostle Paul's words were meant to guide people's treatment of each other in the Christian fellowship, but the advice is good also for conducting rummage sales, of all things! Anyone who comes to your sale is doing you a favor, not vice-versa. We should always be thankful people would take the time to come and visit our garages, yards, or porches. (If, however, someone comes to visit your garage at night when you're not having a sale, go ahead and call the police.)

GO AHEAD AND DO IT

My sister-in-law, Joey, and I throw a rummage sale together almost every summer. If you do not think you are organized enough to have a sale, we are living examples that it can be done. Take comfort, one of our sales was the epitome of poor planning.

Paul took our kids for a short vacation to see some of our family, and Joey came over to our house late Friday night with her items. Joey told me she had only a few things, and so I figured this sale would be a cinch.

Joey pulled up with a car so full of bags and boxes she should have been arrested for driving with her vision to the rear severely obstructed. The accumulation on her back seat was only to be outdone by the amount of stuff she had stuffed into her trunk.

Needless to say, between her storehouse of items and my garage full of clothes and toys and so forth, we were up the entire night pricing, folding, ironing, and above all else, laughing. At 3:00 A.M. we retired to my neighbor's hot tub (I had made arrangements earlier) for a quick break, but other than that we worked until the first rummager showed up at around 7:00 A.M. Fatigue notwithstanding, we had a great time.

Every time we have a sale Joey jumps on me about using the same jokes all day long. What does she expect after not getting any sleep? Besides, when you've got a good thing going—you can have a memory-making experience putting on these sales—even more importantly, you can leave a lasting impression on your visitors throughout your day.

Be a great hostess. Smile, laugh, tell old jokes, put out coffee and doughnuts. (I know food and a good cup of coffee surely puts me in a buying mood!) Keep your eyes open for ways you can be used effectively for Christ. For example, more than once I have been able to give things to people who looked like they were needing more than what they could buy. It's awesome that the Lord can use us even in something as simple as a rummage sale.

Have fun at your sale endeavor and, just in case I am able to come, serve doughnuts.

Journal

ON THE SURFACE ...

1. What do you have a habit of collecting too much of? Examples: Clothes, shoes, dishes, children, and so forth.

_____

2. What is the hardest thing for you to get rid of?

_____

UNDER THE SKIN ...

Jeremiah 17:10
"I the LORD search the heart
  and examine the mind,
to reward a man according to his conduct,
  according to what his deeds deserve."

My house is not the only area where I tend to collect too much stuff if I don't keep a disciplined watch over it. My spiritual life also seems cluttered at times (actually, many times). I imagine Jesus going into the different rooms in my heart and finding offensive pictures tucked away in dark corners from watching a show on TV that I shouldn't have watched. I can easily see him finding heavy books full of notes of how others have wronged me. (I wrote them down in my memory so I wouldn't forget them!) Under my bed he finds hurt feelings that I have swept there because I have chosen not to deal with my anger. (I'll just save it under there where it can grow and fester.) As for my mouth and all the rotten stuff I tend to say—well my guilty lips take up the entire living room and most of the kitchen in my "heart home."

You see, living with too many clothes and toys is one thing; living in disharmony with God is a whole different issue. Take inventory of your spiritual house and see if it might be time to clean out the closets. (Let Jesus throw that junk away. Don't let others store it in their "houses.")

1. If Jesus walked through the rooms of your heart, what would he find in the closets?

_____

_____

_____

_____

2. Do you honestly feel a need to get rid of the sin Jesus might find in your life?

_____

_____

_____

_____

3. Do you consider Jesus big enough (and concerned enough) to get rid of all your sin?

_____

_____

_____

_____

NOW WHAT ...?

1. Write down the hardest area of your spiritual life to keep clean. What is your method of defense against this temptation?

_____

_____

_____

_____

SOMETHING TO PASS ON ...

I do not believe your child needs to know in detail all that you struggle with spiritually, but I do strongly believe that your child can benefit from knowing you do struggle with living for the Lord at times. My oldest child and I have talked a great deal about his mouth. I have told him countless times to be careful with his words. During these conversations I have shared how this is an area I also struggle with. I don't go into great detail because he's too young (plus, he's my child and not my accountability partner), but I think he appreciates knowing that Mom has similar struggles. My challenge to you is to share a basic struggle with your child. If the moment is right, pray about your struggles together. Please remember, though, to keep it light. Don't tell your teenage daughter that you have a problem with lust in regard to her Spanish teacher. That is a little too much information.

·Chapter 4·
PRUDENT
ENTERTAINMENT

> "Little activities that cause us to touch and talk will not be wasted on our children. There are many fun, exciting things to do in our very own backyards."

I love staying home with my kids. I couldn't be happier. If you are a stay-at-home mommy, you will understand what I am about to say. There are mornings that I wake up and am overwhelmed with fear at the thought of having to entertain my two- and four-year-old boys, plus take care of my newborn. It seems as though this could be the very day that they victoriously claim the little amount of sanity that I have left. If I don't plan something, I am irritable, tense, and basically a real drag. Those are not good characteristics for a mommy to possess. They create irritable, tense little kids!

To avoid this possibly ugly day, I like to fill most of my days with at least one thing to look forward to (besides nap time, that is). For me, I need to get out of my house or do something creative at least once a day. That may mean merely going grocery shopping or going for a walk. It may even mean an occasional trip to McDonald's. These little outings and activities help me keep a handle on what I consider to be the toughest job a woman can encounter, being an effective mother.

Now when you consider the mother who works outside the home as well as inside of the home, you throw even more coal on the emotional fire. I hope we can come up with ideas that will work in with your incredible schedule as well.

As I have stated many times already in this book, I don't have the money to whisk my kids off to the zoo or to the museum. I have had to think of some things to do that involve little or no money. I look for ideas that tie in with the seasons of the year and have found several different things to do to prepare the kids and the home for the upcoming season or holiday. Perhaps some of these you already do. Maybe though, you will find one idea that will help some long day ahead of you seem not so long.

"LOOKING FOR PROMISES"

This first activity is probably good for children ages two years to ten years. We call it "looking for promises." This is sort of a scavenger hunt for springtime, fall, or whatever season you are entering. If your kids are old enough, you can send them out by themselves with a sack or go with them into the vast outdoors to hunt for nature items that promise us that spring, summer, fall, or winter, is coming. When they've finished, let each child show off his or her promises. He may find a spring bud, dandelion, or leaf; she a red fall leaf or a beautiful fall flower from the neighbor's garden. Whatever it is, try to take the time to listen carefully to your child, being sure to touch each thing. This is also a wonderful time to tell about God and his promises.

"POPCORN BLANKET"

If you like popcorn as much as my two boys do, this is a great activity for you. We call it the "popcorn blanket" (very imaginative, huh?), and it's good for all ages. If you have really little ones, though, you might want to keep them on your lap.

Spread out a large sheet and have the kids sit around the outside of it so they don't get popped on. Plug in your corn popper and put it in the middle of the sheet. Add your oil and popcorn and leave off the lid. Next instruct the kids to be really quiet so they can hear the popcorn begin to pop. Wait about two minutes and enjoy the quiet ... POP ... POP ... POP!

Your kids will love to watch the popcorn bounce out all across the sheet. I tell my kids to wait until all kernels have popped, and then I move the hot popper and give the dig in signal. Then it is your turn to watch your children scamble all over the sheet filling their cheeks with nice warm popcorn. This is a highly enjoyable activity to do at a small party, or on a rainy day!

"LEAF WAXING"

My favorite season is autumn. I love the cool weather and the beautiful colored trees. That is why this next activity is my favorite. It's called "leaf waxing," and, boy, does it have "memory potential." I know I have a mind full of memories of doing this with my mom and now with my own children. Maybe you do this already, but this is how we do it in my home.

First, get a sack and your children and go for a walk. We live next to a university campus that is filled with big trees, and so we needn't travel far. Perhaps you might need to drive to a nearby park. One year Adam and I went out by ourselves since Ryan was too little. We walked and talked for over an hour. His job was to hold the "official leaf bag," and we both picked out the leaves we liked. I liked the bright yellow, orange, and red ones. Adam was more partial to the brown, holey ones with bug eggs attached to them. It didn't matter; I just loved holding his little hand and strolling the campus. Besides, I threw away the buggy ones later when he wasn't looking!

After your walk, head home and spread the leaves out on the counter. This is a good time to get rid of any unwanted leaves and also this allows the leaves to dry. Wax won't stick to wet leaves. While they dry, fill a pan with water and put a sturdy tin pan on top of it. You want to have the tin pan fit in such a way that it is suspended by its rim. It is sort of a makeshift double boiler. You don't want to allow water to get into the top pan.

Now you're ready to put in a bar of wax. You can buy wax, I imagine, at any grocery store. It's rather inexpensive, and it lasts through many projects. The boiling water in the bottom pan will slowly melt the wax bar in the top pan. When the wax is all liquid, go ahead and start waxing those beautiful leaves.

Take a dry leaf by the stem and dip it into the wax so that both sides get covered. Hold the leaf over the hot pan until all the drips fall, then lay it out on wax paper or newspaper to dry. If your leaves are drying dull, you need to turn the burner up. Continue to do this until all of your gorgeous leaves are waxed and now preserved for several weeks of decorating enjoyment.

I love to scatter them on my mantel, piano, dining table, and such. I also like to give them to friends, teachers, and guests and pretend that I really worked hard. One of my friends even sticks the leaves in her fireplace wreath. The possibilities are endless!

"HOLIDAY DECORATING"

I really enjoy art. If you, however, have trouble distinguishing a pen from a pencil, you might not like to do this next activity. We like to decorate for the coming holidays. For instance, before Easter one year we made butterflies, eggs, and crosses. Quite a combination, I know. I let the kids color each one the way they wanted to, and I colored some, too. This provided a good time to tell the listening ears what the cross meant. I know they don't understand the full meaning of Jesus' crucifixion, but it surely is good to introduce our kids early to such important things as these. I first told Adam about the meaning of the cross almost a year ago, and he still remembers our talk! He has, however, forgotten what I told him this morning at breakfast.

One year, after we got the coloring, glittering, and gluing done, we fastened strings to each creation and stuck the ends of the strings to Adam's bedroom ceiling. He loved to lie in bed with his ceiling fan on and watch his butterflies and crosses spin in circles.

I let the boys decorate their room this way for almost every holiday. It makes their bedrooms feel a little more "homey." I think they also enjoy getting to decorate like a big person. We have done three-foot Valentines, Christmas trees, flowers, and so forth. Be creative, and allow your kids to be creative too!

"MAKE MOMMY BEAUTIFUL"

When you read this next idea you might think my children and I have gone too far for some cheap entertainment! But, hey, there are some days when I'm willing to go a step beyond the normal for some fun. Perhaps you have traveled to this place before with your kids. What am I referring to? The make-up drawer!

I sit on a blanket with a box of my old makeup, a brush, and some hair clips. My little artists then proceed to color me with beautiful shades of lipstick, blush, and eye shadow. Now if I were making myself up, I probably wouldn't use lipstick on my cheeks and eyes, but they like it! The kids complete my new look with a lovely new hair style and sometimes even a fresh coat of fingernail and toenail polish. Oh my, do I look beautiful? No, actually, I look almost frightening, but we sure laugh at the "new" me all the way to the mirror.

For anyone who is wondering, I do wash off the makeup before I venture out into public. Although that would surely provide some prudent entertainment for the people who pass us on the street!

"WHAT A LOVELY DAY FOR A PICNIC"

We have all probably ventured out for a picnic with our kids, and therefore this is not a very original idea, but picnics are so wonderful I just wanted to remind everyone. Sometimes I try to think of something special to do with my kids and completely forget about the obvious "picnic approach." We have picnics frequently in the summer. I like to have them in my backyard or over on the university campus, but the best place for us is at a park. We love to meet some friends there and eat, swing, slide, run, teeter-totter, and throw rocks in the river. By the time we get home the kids may stink like sweat and river water, but, boy, are they worn out! I just love our times at the park.

We have picnics even when it's not summer! We don't have them nearly as often, but every now and again we spread out our blanket in the living room and eat our lunch together on the floor. It's not nearly as fun as in the park, but at least the kids don't stink when we're through.

"THE MALL RIDERS"

In my town, Anderson, Indiana, we have a nice little mall. Many people go there every day to walk. When Ryan was just a baby and I was hankering to get out, especially in the winter, I'd pack a little bike for Adam to ride and we'd head to the mall. We traveled all over the mall and had a very relaxing time. The older people who walk the mall got such a kick out of seeing Adam zooming along on his little bike. Many people said, "What a great idea!"

One day when Ryan was a little older, we took their big Little Tykes car. That day a woman came up to me and said, "We (she was with friends) think you should get an award for letting your kids bring that little car here. They will never forget such a special time." Now, I didn't realize it was such a big deal as all that, but it surely was fun. It also allowed me to do a little shopping without wondering where my boys were. It's hard to miss a big yellow car!

Another problem I faced going from one to two children after Ryan was born was I didn't know where to put Adam when I went to the grocery. He didn't like sitting on those hard wire racks under the cart for very long, and so I had the privilege of chasing him and threatening him while trying to plan meals for the week. In hopes of giving him something to do, I let him take his little bike to the grocery. It worked out just great. He rode alongside my cart and then up and down my aisle while I shopped. Also, his little mischievous hands were too busy steering to put any food in the cart.

Let me add to this that Anderson is a relatively small town. Our mall and our grocery are small enough that I feel safe to do such things. I wouldn't suggest this activity if you fear your child would drive way ahead of you or get lost in a crowd.

"A HOT IDEA FOR A COLD DAY"

I really hate winter. I know that's not nice, but I really do. I like it up to Christmas, and then I think there should be a law against snow. You can't go out and play for very long with toddlers when it's cold. Besides, it takes just as long to get my children ready to face the outside as it takes for the errand I have to run. I just don't care for the cold, however, since the ice and snow keep on coming, I especially like to plan something for those long winter days inside.

If you have a wood burning fireplace, versus a gas fireplace, try this. Have a marshmallow roast using a bent coat hanger. If you happen to have graham crackers and chocolate, make some Smores. Oh, that sounds so good! Or if it is lunch time, roast hot dogs on your indoor campfire. Can't you just see your little family huddled around the fire roasting goodies? This could even be a dinner that could be prepared without much effort from good old mom! These things are so simple, but so special. It almost makes me wish today were cold and snowy. (*Not!*)

Have you ever been with anyone who has said something like this? "Kids today are not like they used to be." That statement is usually followed by a whole stream of condemning remarks about how kids have somehow changed over the years. Do you know how I feel about this? I believe kids who are born today are of the same quality as children born one hundred, two hundred, three hundred years ago. What has changed is not the children; it's our society.

We as parents are quick to buy television games to entertain children for hours. We don't make it a priority to play and eat together. Grandparents tend to move away and retire where it's sunny, instead of playing a consistently active part in the molding of the next generation. I don't mean to come down on anyone; I'm only trying to make my point that our youth have not mysteriously lost their values over the years. We have just forgotten that it is our responsibility to instill and teach those precious values. Little activities that cause us to touch and talk will not be wasted on our children. There are many fun, exciting things to do in our very own backyards. By being imaginative, and downright silly at times, you can get to know that young person in your life a little better. Take the time today, no matter what your schedule or pocketbook says, and make some memories. Making memories—now that's a prudent idea!

Journal

ON THE SURFACE ...

1. What is your favorite memory of a special time with one of your parents or grandparents?

_____

_____

_____

_____

_____

2. When is the last time you sat down, really looked into the eyes of your child and giggled?

_____

_____

_____

_____

_____

UNDER THE SKIN ...

Read Psalm 119. I love this very long chapter because it is a love letter to God. The psalmist can't get enough of God. He studies God's word (verse 11). He meditates on God's word (verse 15). On and on throughout this chapter you will find this man "ga-ga" over God. He loves to be in an intimate relationship with his Maker.

If we are to pass on a heritage of godly values, we had better be living and experiencing those values ourselves. Our children not only need time with us; our children also need us to spend time with our God.

2. How important would your child say God is to you? What would he or she use as a scale to weigh that amount? (Example: I see my mom praying and reading her Bible every morning in the living room when I get up, and so I know God is really important to her.)

_____

_____

_____

_____

3. If you were guaranteed that your child would have the exact relationship with God that you do, would you be happy?

_____

_____

_____

NOW WHAT ...?

In your journal write down some goals you have for your relationship with God this week. Share them with a friend who will hold you accountable to those goals.

SOMETHING TO PASS ON ...

Ask your child if he or she would like to go for a walk. If you have more than one child, take a separate walk with each one. Try to walk where there will be few distractions so that you can focus on each other.

Journal

· Chapter 5 ·
AN EYE
FOR FASHION

> "Let's be encouraged to approach each decorating job, as with all things, in a spirit of prayer."

One reason I love my God is because he's huge! God is so awesome that the Maker can create an entire universe in six days (Genesis 1—2). He's so tremendous that he can control the winds and rain (Mark 4:35–41). He's so powerful that he can bring a dead man back to life (John 11:43–44). Yet he's so gentle that he knows me intimately and loves me as his very own daughter. It's because of this love that I know he cares about my "big" needs, just as he cares about my "little" needs.

When I have a project in my house that I want to do, I pray about it. I pray that I will find the right materials at good prices. I pray that God will guide me as I work. I also ask him to help the project turn out well. Maybe you think it is futile to pray about things such as household decorating, but I believe that our God not only hears those prayers but answers them as well. After all, let's not forget how much God loves to decorate!

Exodus 35—40 is filled with very detailed orders, from God to Moses, concerning the tabernacle God wanted built. God instructed Moses about the materials, the size, and the color with which he wanted everything made. He ordered the people to bring gold, silver, and bronze; blue, purple, and scarlet yarn; and fine linen. The Israelites gave gems and precious stones to be used. They brought skins of animals, beautiful wood, and so much more. Oh! It had to have been so gorgeous! After everything was made, God went on for another chapter telling Moses how he wanted everything set up. Now that's a God who has an eye for fashion!

It is important to me that I remind you of these things. Philippians 4:6 and 1 Thessalonians 5:16–18 tell us to pray about everything and to be thankful in all circumstances. Let's be encouraged to approach each decorating job, as with all things, in a spirit of prayer. So as you read these next ideas, if you see any that strike you, pray about them. Or perhaps, pray that the Lord will give you your own idea.

My very favorite rooms to decorate are my children's rooms. When I first found out I was pregnant with Adam, I could hardly think of anything but his nursery. Border? Wallpaper? Pink or blue paint? Pictures? I didn't know what I wanted. Finally, I decided I wanted to go with the Noah's ark theme. I started searching for the perfect border.

After I found what I liked, I considered the cost. Once again my frugality kicked in. I thought, "Oh, I hate to think of spending that much money. Maybe I could paint those up there". Yes, folks, I did. I painted arks, animals, rainbows, whales, and waves until I thought I'd pass out. I painted, standing on a chair, clear up to my due date. I love to paint though, and so I found it fun. (At least it was fun for the first twenty-five arks, then it became annoying.) You might be saying, "You're losing me here, Missy." Well, don't leave me yet.

I have come up with several ideas for decorating bedrooms for children from their infancy to their teen years. To be honest, all of them require you to do some level of painting. That is because paint is really the cheapest way to make a big difference in a bedroom. Most of these ideas call for very little painting skill. I am sure that you can do most of these if you make an attempt.

THE SMALL CHILD'S ROOM

Here's an idea that would be good from newborn through seven-year-olds. It's a hand print theme. First, measure from the floor up, about four feet. Put a dot on the wall. Continue around the room, and then draw a line connecting the dots. It would be so cute to paint the bottom a different color than the top, perhaps red on bottom, white on top.

Next, you will need to buy three or so different colors of paint. You could buy craft paint in the little bottles; however, if you do buy this paint you need to remember it will not be scrubbable. Sometimes, to save money when I need a lot of different colors, I buy some white scrubbable paint, pour out just enough into a dish, and then add my own colors from the little craft paints. Make sure whatever you use is latex. It will be much easier to remove from little wiggly fingers.

Pour a pool of paint out on a plastic plate. Then you need to find at least one child and dip his or her little hand in the paint, being careful not to "overload." Have the youngster carefully press that hand on the wall, with the palm about one inch above the line. Don't worry if the handprints are not perfectly straight. "Cockeyed" prints add character. You could even use a couple of different sized hands. If you can sew, you could buy fabric paints and repeat the hand prints on material to use for curtains and a bed coverlet.

Here is another idea that is very easy. Buy or cut sponges in different shapes. Dip them in bright or pastel colors of paint and decorate your walls. To make big footballs, basketballs, baseballs, whatever, just sponge the basic shape of the ball on the wall. Next use a black paint pen and draw in the lines of the ball stitches. Easy! I am sure kids would even enjoy their ceiling covered in interesting shapes. I know I would like to sponge paint different kinds of cheesecake on my bedroom ceiling. Oh, the dreams I could have....

A LITERARY THEME

This next idea does require a little more careful painting. I did this for Adam's first "big boy" room. I wanted to do something really different; dare I say—loud? It needed to be something that just shouted fun. Adam loves Sesame Street so I decided to paint his favorite characters up on his walls. I took books containing Sesame Street characters to guide me as I sketched the figures up on the wall, making the characters very big. It didn't take too long, and, once again, I really enjoyed doing it.

There are other possibilities to get this done if you would like to do it but do not care for drawing freehand. You can photocopy from books or magazines onto transparencies just about anything that tickles the fancy of your child. Then see if you can borrow from your church an overhead projector for a day. Simply project onto the wall the transparency you've made, and trace it. You can paint the tracing after you've returned the projector. Or you could even find someone to do the sketching for you. If you have a friend who can paint well, trade her for something you can do—perhaps floral arranging, cleaning, baby sitting, or cooking dinner for her and her family. I know all of those sound very good to me!

As I have already shared, I have two boys. I almost always do projects for them in bold primary colors. So when my husband and I found out that we were expecting a baby girl, I went pink crazy! I looked forward to transforming Ryan's very boyish nursery into a VERY girlish nursery. I looked at many different fabrics until I found the perfect print. Oh, it was beautiful! Pink and cream bouquets of flowers ran in big wide stripes. I could not help but daydream of how lovely it would be in the nursery.

All this beauty would be available for only $20.00 a yard. Well, now, whom was I kidding? I carried that mental picture and dream for about a month. I finally realized that even if I were to get it on sale I still couldn't afford to make curtains, a comforter, bed skirt, bumper pad, and the like. I really believe the

Lord was showing me, very gently, that this was not a prudent plan. I kept rationalizing it as prudent because I would be doing all my sewing. Slowly, however, I gave in to what I believe the Lord wanted me to hear. Material that cost twenty dollars a yard might very well be prudent for someone with more money, but there are many more things for which I could use this money. I knew God would help me come up with something equally wonderful as my first plan, but for a price I could afford.

Sure enough, as I was thinking of other ideas for this book, a very simple idea popped into my head. It was to make dolls going all around the room touching hands. Every doll looked different. Some very fancy, some plain. Dolls with different skin and hair colors. I mean to tell you, I had a whole room planned in just minutes, complete with what kind of fabric to use and everything. I decided to try it in my nursery if the prices were right. The material I wanted now ran about $2.50. I asked the saleslady if it would be going on sale soon, and sure enough, just a few days later, I got it for $1.50 a yard. That was a far cry from $20.00 a yard!

As soon as I could, I got busy with the painting. Three of the walls were covered with bulletin board. I tore those down only to discover that they were being held up by a black tar glue. I was sick, wondering how we would ever get it off the walls. Paul, my hero, scraped and sanded. Then he filled in the cracks and holes with Spack. More sanding and a good coat of primer were required. Finally, the walls were ready for me. I painted the top part of the walls white, and all of my bottom paneling got a fresh coat of pink! Then I cut the stencil I wanted. I took a strong piece of paper and drew around a cup for a nice round head. A triangle made a good body, and then some simple arms and legs completed my pattern. After cutting her out, she was ready to go! I put her toes on the line of my paneling and traced the stencil over and over so that each doll touched hands with another. I had to be careful not to lose part of the doll at the end of the wall. Sometimes I shortened a couple of the dolls' arms slightly to make them fit in the room's dimensions.

Now for the fun part! As I tell you how I painted these dolls, please don't start to feel you couldn't do it. If you think this would work in your daughter's bedroom I hope you will try it. Each step is so easy. Start on a wall you won't notice much. By the time you get to the main visual wall you will be a pro!

Anyway, after they were stenciled on the wall (with pencil) I "blocked" them in. This means I painted them with a basic color, no details. I chose to do different skin colors. Then I "blocked" in their dresses, and painted all their shoes black.

Hair of every style began to form on the tops of their round heads. Ponytails, short, long, braids, brushed, and tangled. Every doll got a hairdo!

Next, I painted little pink circles on each cheek. For the eyes, nose, and mouth I used a black paint pen. The time this pen saved me was wonderful. Sometimes I colored in pink lips, but not on everyone. After outlining everything, the doll was just about done. I used my glue gun to add ribbons to some and pearl necklaces to others. (Don't add anything too small that a baby could pull down and choke on.) I also used wallpaper glue to stick a couple of cloth dresses on some of the dolls. The ribbons, necklaces, and cloth dresses gave a three-dimensional effect. Finally I was all done! I know it sounds like a lot of work, but this will last my daughter for a long time.

I finished the room off with curtains and other baby needs that I sewed with my $1.50 material. I found a floral print to pull everything together for $2.99. I had an old dresser that had pathetic looking drawers. I tried to sand the drawers and paint them, but they were too far gone. I had bought the dresser at a rummage sale for a dollar, and so what was I to expect? However, it was such a sturdy old thing that I decided to salvage it.

I cut pieces of my material to fit the drawers. I covered each drawer with wallpaper paste and laid my material down on top of it. Smoothing the material on nice and straight was an easy task. I put the drawers outside to dry and then gave them a coat of spray varnish. Later I covered each with a coat of polyurethane. A couple of staples made sure that with all its use the material would stay in place. Brass handles were added to help take some of the abuse. My old dresser now looks new. Everything I did in Madison's room was very inexpensive. I am sure I paid between $75.00—$100.00 for the whole room. I think that's pretty prudent. Also, it's nice to know that I did it myself; however, if Madison Joanna turns out to be a boy, we're moving!

A TEENAGER'S ROOM

If you have teenagers to decorate for, it can be just as easy. Let them help you decide on how to do it. Spend a little time in prayer about it with them. Once you decide together, let them help. This creates instant family time! If you need some help on ideas, let me give you a couple.

Around the middle of each wall take a pencil and make a zigzag line connecting all around the room, sort of like a crack around an egg. Paint the top half one color and the bottom another. You could even go a step further. Above the first line make a second line, six or more inches above it. Paint that middle strip another color.

You're looking at a very minimal expense. You could do it with soft wavy lines or jagged ones. Just have fun. Remember this is your child's room. Let teenagers use their imagination to make it a place to which they are proud to bring their friends.

Well, there are a few ideas and procedures for decorating. It's amazing what a little paint and time can do for a room, not to mention for the disposition of your child. I know I am a lot happier in a pretty room. I remember when I was about ten years old, I had a bedroom that would have never made it into a Better Homes magazine. It was about two feet by three feet, and the walls were dark paneling. My carpet was orange, red, and brown speckled. Oh, stars! It was bad. If you don't feel sorry for me yet, let me tell you the final straw.

It had no windows! It started out to be my two brothers' room; however, as you can imagine, a little room with no ventilation housing two growing boys, was bordering on a health hazard. The smells that lurked in that room still bring tears to my eyes. Consequently, mom and dad had the boys pack up their stink and move to a room with a window. After I lived in there a couple of years (it took that long to air it out), my parents decided it was time to redecorate. Maybe I sound a little corny, but when my mom and dad decided I needed a change of scenery, I was ecstatic. They painted my brown walls white. They painted my orange dressers white with beautiful blue drawers, and I even got a new floor of blue carpet. They bought me the bedspread of my choice (within reason), which happened to be a white bedspread with blue and yellow butterflies. The fabric was so slippery I could slide right across it!

Because I didn't have any windows, they were going to buy matching curtains to put on the wall for color. I suggested we hang them in front of the bed, and they did it! They hung them on rods from my ceiling and pulled them gracefully over to the wall. The curtains were long enough to almost touch the floor. It made my bed look so pretty. After we hung pictures, butterflies, and some adhesive mirrors, it was like paradise! I remember thinking that my parents surely must love me to do such a wonderful thing. I don't even think I asked them to do it. What a difference a nice bedroom can make!

How about brightening up your child's space? Don't be afraid of doing it yourself. Look around for the best prices, and remember to be prudent in all your decorating decisions. Most of all remember to pray. Pray to our Father who cares about every detail in our lives. "Cast all your anxiety on him because he cares for you" (1 Peter 5:7). Isn't God great to love us so completely?

Journal

ON THE SURFACE ...

1. When you were little, what would your "dream bedroom" have looked like? How about now?

_____

_____

_____

2. Would you prefer to spend your extra money (if there is such a thing) on paint for a new project in your house or would you rather spend it on a big gallon of ice cream and eat it in your house? (Have you ever had that peanut butter ice cream with the big hunks of chocolate in it? OH MY!)

_____

_____

_____

UNDER THE SKIN ...

1 Peter 5:7 says, "Cast all your anxiety on him because he cares for you."

_____

_____

_____

1. Do you think it is almost demeaning to God when you bring him your little concerns such as how to decorate your kitchen or what car to buy? Why or why not?

_____

_____

_____

2. Do you feel that you will wear God out if you come to him with too much, that you should save coming to him with only the big stuff?

_____

_____

_____

I can't say that I don't struggle with both of these questions. Sometimes I wonder if God says, "Missy, I don't care if you paint your kitchen green or not!" At times I wonder if calling upon the Almighty for something as small and insignificant as my household decor would cause God not to be as quick to listen to my bigger requests. But the verse we just read says to cast all my anxieties on God. Why? Because he cares for me. My world that I live in basically consists of my house. I spend a great deal of time here; therefore, I place a great deal of importance on what color the walls are. I believe that makes it important to my Father. If Madison comes to me with one of her baby dolls and is concerned because its little dress won't fit over its big head, that is a concern I will address— not because I care about that little baby doll, but because Madison is my child and I love her. Give your concerns to God. He will care—because he cares for you.

NOW WHAT ...?

Write down the top five things that concern you right now. Give them to the Lord.

_____

_____

_____

_____

_____

SOMETHING TO PASS ON ...

Ask each of your children to tell you their top three concerns and pray about those together too. Save them! Someday they might be really funny.

Journal

Journal

· Chapter 6 ·
PRUDENT IN YOUR PLENTY

> "I have to find ways to save.... Ruth's lifestyle allows her to meet needs of other people."

I had just had child number three, Madison Joanna Jansen, when I found myself overweight, overworked, and overwhelmed. I didn't feel good about myself, and all those feelings were rubbing off into other areas of my life. Yes, I believe that being a child of God is enough to make me a masterpiece, but that doesn't get me into my "prechildren" clothes anymore!

Since she had lost quite a bit of weight, one of my sweetest friends gave me some of her clothes to wear until I could get back into my own stuff. My favorite was a green outfit with big jewels imprinted around the neck and at the ankles. It fit, and I felt good in it—that is, for about one month. After that, I hated that outfit! Every time I had to go somewhere nice, I headed for my closet to put on "Old Faithful." Paul and I would laugh as I walked to my room, saying, "Gee, Honey, guess what I'm going to put on!"

One Sunday morning I tried on a few things, hoping to find that they would fit. Instead I found myself standing defeated in a pile of clothes that just lay there laughing at me. I looked in my closet, and there it was: "Old Faithful." It seemed to be smirking and taunting me, "Ha, Ha, I knew you'd be back!" I couldn't help myself; I cried.

I knew my friends at church were noticing. After all, a girl who consistently walks in late wearing a bright green, jewel-covered outfit for six weeks straight is sure to be found out. One of my friends joked, "Well, Missy, did you get a new outfit?" I laughed, but I knew I would either have to lose weight in the next week or catch a nasty cold so I could stay home the next Sunday.

When I got home, I ate a big bowl of ice cream while I decided. Maybe the cold spoon would give me the sniffles. The thing that bothered me the most was that Paul was having his ten year high school reunion soon, and I knew I'd show up wearing you-know-what!

Then came Ruth. Ruth is one of my friends at church. She always has a funny line to say, and even more intriguing, she is always dressed in head-to-toe fashion. While my nails are stained with whatever painting project I'm working on, Ruth's are painted to coordinate with her shoes and handbag! I can't stand it. If only she smelled like spit-up or something! Fashion advice, however, isn't all Ruth has to offer. You can find Ruth wherever you find someone with a need. Ruth is so unselfish and giving. She is truly a wonderful person whose heart is as gold as her shoes. Let me tell you how she touched my life with an example of prudent living I will never forget.

Try to picture this scene, or perhaps you have lived it and it's all too familiar. I am grocery shopping with my three children, Moe, Larry, and Curly. One is making a Kool-Aid run, one is hanging on my leg, and the last is hungry and crying because her newborn mind can't understand why mommy won't nurse her right there in aisle nine. After all, it is the dairy section!

Into all this chaos comes Ruth. Ruth's children are in school, but the look of sympathy in her eyes tells me she remembers a similar time. She takes Maddy and calms her while I gather the other two, and soon things are a little more under control.

"Missy, you know I've been thinking," says Ruth. "I'd like to take you out for lunch sometime. Just you and Madison. I'll get baby sitters for the boys, and we'll shop, go to lunch, and have a great day!" It sounded like a dreamy plan to me, but to be honest I didn't know if it would ever happen since both of our schedules are so busy. Well, within a couple of days Ruth had everything planned. She had baby sitters for the boys and a schedule for us. She refused my offer to pay for anything, including lunch. I could hardly wait until the big day!

Finally, it came. Ruth arrived on time and looking sharp. She helped me get the boys ready, and off we went. On our way, Ruth's usual light-hearted voice turned serious as she said, "Now, Missy, I want you to listen to me. I want to do something for you today. I've been praying about it, and I just really want to take you shopping today."

As my mouth dropped to the floor, she continued with tears in her eyes, "If I bought you a couple of outfits, would that hurt Paul's feelings?"

I said, "Well, no, Ruth, but you shouldn't buy me anything...."

She cut me off by saying, "Now I don't want you to fight me on this, or I can't do it!" She told me of money she had for days such as this, and that it would be a special time for her, too. She told me not to tell anyone; this was just our secret. (That's why I'm writing it in a book! Ha!) Ruth told me that she noticed that I wasn't feeling very good about myself lately (she probably was sick of the green outfit, too), and she just wanted to take me out and spoil me. I was embarrassed, but willing to make the sacrifice. (Oh, all right, spoil me!)

Our first stop was a boutique. I told Ruth about Paul's reunion, and she was amazed at the Lord's timing. She said I'd need a fancy outfit. I tried on some clothes that weren't even on sale! It was quite an experience. After a couple of hours we stopped for lunch in a quaint little restaurant, and then we were off again. Conversation flows easily with Ruth, and money flows from her pocketbook. By the end of the day I had grown quite friendly with this spoiling business, and it hurt my pride less with each purchase. I went home that night with several outfits, earrings, and two new pairs of shoes.

I couldn't decide whether to cry or parade down the street in my new attire. Paul teased me about my new improved attitude. I had been spoiled by a woman who had the means to do it. As I told her how much it meant to me, Ruth looked at me and said, "I've had a fantastic day that I will never forget. I've had just as much fun as you." I doubted that, but she was surely sincere. I went to the reunion not long after that fun day. I went feeling good about myself, and I didn't have on anything green. It felt great!

Ruth gave me an example that day of a completely different prudent lifestyle. My life, right now, calls for a prudence different than Ruth's. I have to find ways to save money. That's not always easy. Ruth's lifestyle allows her to meet needs of other people. A lot of times that calls for her to spend money. That's not always easy, either. Ruth has learned how not to be selfish with all the Lord has given her.

Remember the definition for prudent: "Exercising sound judgment in practical matters"? Ruth's witness to me will help me to distinguish between prudently hanging on to my money and prudently giving my money away.

First Peter 5:2–4 says: "Be shepherds of God's flock that is under your care, serving as overseers—not because you must, but because you are willing, as God wants you to be; not greedy for money, but eager to serve; not lording it over those entrusted to you, but being examples to the flock. And when the Chief Shepherd appears, you will receive the crown of glory that will never fade away." Enjoy your crown, Ruth!

Journal

ON THE SURFACE ...

1. What does your favorite outfit look like? How often do you wear it?

_____

_____

2. How much would you as a family have to make a year for you to consider the amount to be enough?

_____

UNDER THE SKIN ...

I love the Proverbs. They make me laugh, think, and examine. The Proverbs are full of wise thoughts about money. Here are just a few:

Proverbs 11:24
"One man gives freely, yet gains even more;
   another withholds unduly, but comes to poverty."

Proverbs 11:25
"A generous man will prosper;
   he who refreshes others will himself be refreshed."

Proverbs 15:6
"The house of the righteous contains great treasure,
   but the income of the wicked brings them trouble."

1. How much would your family have to make a year for you to consider the amount to be enough to give some of it away?

2. Would you rather give away your time or your money? Why?

_____

_____

NOW WHAT ...?

One day several years ago I remember going to Bible study and saying that I didn't have enough money to buy stamps. (Why in the world did I tell them that? Sometimes I wonder about myself.) When I got home a book of stamps was stuck in my door. Now at that time a whole book of stamps couldn't have cost too much money, but whoever did that really was a blessing to me that day. My point is, a gift of giving doesn't have to be expensive. Just be willing to refresh others and God will refresh you as well.

SOMETHING TO PASS ON ...

I will never forget the Christmas when I was a child and my family bought presents for needy families. We wrapped them all up and went out on Christmas Eve and delivered them. I can still see my dad sneak up to the door, ring the doorbell, and then make a mad dash for the car.

How about getting involved in something like that this Christmas? Or, plan for some other fun way of giving. Your child, no matter what age, will learn a great deal from experiences such as these. By the way, I could use some stamps.

·Chapter 7·
ONLY A SEASON

> "I don't think that every bad mood that comes along to us parents excuses us from playing and getting on with life, but I do believe when there are days that we just can't shake off a sense of misery. [Sometimes we need] a time-out."

"I know it's hard sometimes," a caring, well-meaning mother with grown children says, "but don't forget, this is only a season of your life." That is great advice, and I honestly appreciate hearing it, but I want to say, "Well then, I hope this is the winter!" Mothers of teenagers probably would claim the "teen years" as winter, but all I know is it feels pretty cold and dreary around here somedays.

As I said before, I stay home with my children, and I absolutely adore it. I thank the Lord for that privilege, but there are days that I think if some little short kid calls me "Mommy" in that obnoxious, needy voice just one more time, I'm going to lose my mind. Some may argue that I already have lost my mind!

You might wonder why I am painting this ugly picture of motherhood. I don't think of this as ugly, just realistic. I have read several books where the mommy talks as if she can't possibly get enough of her children. Let me state this very clearly: I CAN get enough of my children. That does not mean I love them less than a mother who won't suggest she feels this way; I'm just more honest! There comes a time in every day (or more than once) when I really need to spend time by myself.

I can't help but think how frustrating it must be for mothers who work all day filling the needs of their employers and then have to go home and immediately start filling the needs of their families. It would even be more exhausting to be a single parent and not have the support (whether it be physical or emotional help) of a spouse.

I know the stress has to be overwhelming at times for parents who work under such strain. That is why I want to commit this chapter to ideas, new and old, to use with your children when you need a break.

Even though my kids know that I love to play with them, they also know that I can't play any and every time they want. I let them know that there is work that I have to do before I can play. They also know that there are times that, frankly, mommy really doesn't want to play. There isn't a thing in the world wrong with needing some time to ourselves, Mom or Dad, but there are ways to convey that need to our children without hurting their feelings. The first thing we need to do is recognize when we need a break.

One Monday morning I got up feeling yucky. It was the day after a holiday, which always leaves me a little blue. I was being visited by the "Monthly Monster" and experiencing the discomfort that "It" brings. Basically, I felt like staying in bed. Unfortunately, that just can't happen. I got up and gave Madison her bottle, got the boys their breakfast, and ate my own breakfast. Then I got Maddy dressed, got the boys dressed, and got myself dressed. By this time I thought maybe it was time for naps, but to my dismay it was only 8:30 A.M.

Well, with the whole day ahead of us I figured I had better make the most of it as I tried to escape into the bathroom and clean a toilet or two. Adam found me and asked if I would take them out to fly their new kites. I love to fly kites, and I love my children, and so even though I was feeling emotionally close to the edge of a cliff, I decided to take them. To tell you the truth, I thought it would be easier to fly a dumb kite than take the time and effort to say no and hear all the whining that would take place. So I stuck Maddy in the stroller, put coats on the kids (it was really cold), got myself bundled up, and we went over to the field across the street. All the way there Adam talked. I mean that child can ramble on and on. Sometimes I just watch his little mouth going and going, and I am amazed at his endurance. Anyway, all the way there he kept talking and telling me jokes that I never understood.

Finally, we made our way to the middle of the field. Ryan was quiet the whole way, partly because this was a new kind of outing for him, partly because he couldn't get a word in edgewise. I told him I would get his kite up first. I took his Batman kite in my skillful hand and I ran across the field as fast as I could while bundled up in my winter coat. As I ran I noticed four things that were pushing me closer and closer to the edge of my emotional cliff.

Number one: As I ran, the kite was practically dragging behind me. That, by the way, is not a good kite flying technique.

Number two: I was barely moving. I was trying to run fast, but my fast wasn't fast anymore. I started to feel embarrassed.

Number three: As I ran, I heard Ryan running after me, crying and screaming, "That's my kite, Mommy! I want to fly my kite!" I stopped running for a minute (which wasn't hard since the word "running" is a great exaggeration to what I was really doing), and said something like, "Ryan I am just trying to get this kite in the air, then I will let you fly it. And if you don't stop crying I am just going to keep this kite and fly it myself!" Now, wasn't that a smart thing to say to a little two-year-old boy whose only problem is he doesn't understand what's going on?

Number four: The entire time I was "running" with my arm up in the air trying to get this ugly kite to soar up into the heavens, Adam in all his wisdom was running beside me telling me how he was going to get his own kite up and what exactly I needed to do to get Ryan's up better. Finally, in exasperation I exclaimed, "Adam, be quiet!" I jumped. I not only jumped I leaped off my emotional cliff. I had had it with my kids, the weather, the kites, my period, my big coat, my athletic abilities, my life! I tried to be calm and polite as I said that the wind was just not strong enough, and we would have to try again later. What a flop.

Do you know, though, what the problem with that outing really was? It never should have happened! I should have stayed home and avoided the whole thing. Instead I went and said hurtful things to my kids and pushed myself too far emotionally that morning. Now, don't get me wrong, I don't think that every bad mood that comes along to us parents excuses us from playing and getting on with life, but I do believe that there are days when we just can't shake off a sense of misery. It's just too big for the moment. Take fifteen minutes or so to relax, pray, read, clean, whatever.

That Monday morning was one of those times when I needed to have a "time-out." It reminds me of Proverbs 22:3: "A prudent man sees danger and takes refuge, but the simple keep going and suffer for it." I really should have taken refuge.

Whenever we realize we need a break, let's just take one, right? Oh, if only it were that easy. Before we can relax sometimes we need to arrange for the kids to have something to do. Most of the time my kids will just play with their toys, but other times they might need something special to keep them busy. Let me share some of my ideas with you.

THE "ASK MOMMY" DRAWER

One day last summer I was driving down the road when my eyes caught sight of an old 50s-style stove sitting out by the curb. Its white surfaces were yellowed, and the knobs were off, but it was so cute! I asked the man of the house if I could take it, and he very happily agreed. I took it home and scrubbed it up. Oh, I love it! It now sits in my dining room with very little purpose other than to add charm and to hold my napkins and such. It does have one very important drawer. It's called the "Ask Mommy" drawer. Inside this drawer you will find such treasures as glitter, paints, markers, stamps, glue, and so forth. Nobody is allowed to get in the "Ask Mommy" drawer without permission. When I need to take refuge for a few minutes the kids can get in that drawer and create several masterpieces all by themselves. We all have a nice time. Three cheers for the "Ask Mommy" drawer!

BAKED BISCUIT ART

Surely, we all have refrigerated biscuits sitting in our refrigerators from time to time. The next time you would like to do something without the kids at your ankles, sit them at the table and give them some refrigerated biscuits. Tell them about a holiday coming up and challenge them to make something with that theme. Let them sit and shape the dough like playdough for a while, then put their creations on a cookie sheet and bake them. The kids will love to eat their artwork. You could even have them do this project while you cook dinner and then serve their biscuits to the whole family.

ROOM CLEANING FUN

One of the great things about little kids is that they don't know yet that cleaning is a drag. To a child, everything is fun! So enjoy it while you can, and let them "help" you clean. If I have something I need to do without the children, there are several jobs I let them do. Cleaning their room is something for which they need to be responsible. I realize that a four-year-old and a two-year-old have some tasks, such as making a bed, that will still be too much for them, and so my kids have specific jobs that we all know they can handle.

One job is to pick up all the dirty clothes and put them in the clothes hamper. They also have to put all their blankets up on their bed, and all their toys in their toy boxes. Sometimes Adam does attempt bed making, and he is always proud of his efforts. So is Mommy! The greatest thing about sending two little ones off to clean their room is that nine times out of ten they will start picking up their toys but then start playing with those toys, thus creating more time for mommy to do what she needs to do, even if that may be relaxing!

BATHROOM CLEANING DOS AND DON'TS

Another fun room to clean is the bathroom. Our boys' bath is tiled on the floor and on most of the walls. I save old cleaning bottles, and after washing them I fill them with water. It's good to add something with a little smell or color such as vanilla or vinegar. They each take a rag and a squirt bottle back to the bathroom, and away they clean! They really feel proud to do such grown-up work. Make sure your kids know, though, that they can only use a cleaner when mommy gives it to them. Obviously, there are some that can be harmful. Personally, I try to stay away from as many cleaning solutions as I can, just to be safe.

FUN WITH VACUUMING

My Adam is old enough, I feel, to help me vacuum. I plug it in for him and, I mean to tell you, he really goes to it! He sweeps under furniture, rugs, and toys. Even I have never attempted that. I have noticed, however, that he thinks its cool to see the vacuum suck up bigger objects, such as one of his siblings, but in general he does awesome work. Adam gets a look on his face that shows he is excited about being trusted with new things. Hmmm. If only he could learn to cook dinner.

If you don't feel good about a vacuum, give your child a broom to sweep the kitchen or even the porch. You will be surprised at how well children do. Make sure to smother them with praise and kisses for doing such a grown-up task. They will be eager to try it again later.

WAXING, WASHING, AND WATER PLAY

There are other things to let your child clean. My kids love to help me wax furniture. I spray, and they wipe (and then I rewipe). Really, just about any job can be shared with your kids. It's good they know that we all have responsibilities. Some are more fun than others.

One of the things my kids love to do by themselves in the summer is have a car wash. We bring out all their riding toys and line them up in the yard. I give them a big bucket of warm soapy water and two rags. They take turns (I should say they're supposed to take turns) spraying the clean bikes with the hose to rinse them off. This is not only a good way to keep your kids occupied, but it's also good to have clean toys. Warning: children will get wet in this process. Bathing suits are a good idea. Also, any stickers that are on toys sometimes can get damaged by the water.

Since we are talking about water, I like to fill up a basin with water and put it on a towel in the kitchen and let the kids play in it with toys and utensils. It's a very simple yet very effective busy activity.

Those are some ideas to add to your list of ways to occupy your children. Let me say again that kids are wonderful. If you are able to spend time with your kids, whether it be all day or only part of your day, you are truly blessed by the Lord. My children have taught me so much about love, not only how much or how perfectly I am capable of loving them, but how much God must love me.

Children are a gift! Children are also exhausting, and that is why I felt I needed to write this chapter. We provide activities for our kids not because we should try to occupy their time with so much stuff that we won't have to mess with them, but so we can make the most of the time we have together. If you are feeling "blue" or even very busy, then these ideas will give you enough time to put yourself or house back together so you can again be an effective, prudent parent. I'm feeling so much better now, I believe I'm ready to fly a kite!

Journal

ON THE SURFACE ...

1. What drives you to the edge of your emotional cliff faster than anything else?

_____

_____

2. What is your favorite way to relax?

_____

_____

UNDER THE SKIN ...

Isaiah 58:11
"The LORD will guide you always;
  he will satisfy your needs in a sun-scorched land
  and will strengthen your frame.
You will be like a well-watered garden,
  like a spring whose waters never fail."

In my Bible beside this verse I have written in black letters, "My verse as a Mommy". I sometimes feel so worn down and depleted that I consider my home to be a "sun-scorched land". Even my spiritual life can be so dehydrated that I don't have the energy or even the desire to go and be replenished. Pick yourselves up you hot, parched, thirsty Mommys! Go to the Man with the tall glass of cool water. Retreat in His shade and pray. Nourish yourself on sustaining promises such as this verse. God will not only carry you He will also strengthen your frame. But you need to go to Him. I can just see you at the end of a particularly hard day crawling your way across the carpet of your own sun-scorched land saying in a desperate thirsty voice—"water". God will meet you there, I promise. More important—*He* promises.

1. Look up Psalm 121:7 and Psalm 139:7–10. What promise do these verses offer you?

_____

_____

2. What, if anything, is good about coming before the Lord feeling so needy?

_____

_____

NOW WHAT ...?

Next time you feel worn out with your family or work go back and read the list you made from chapter 1. Remember it? Read back through all the "little praises" you found.

SOMETHING TO PASS ON ...

Next time you see that your child is feeling particularly "parched", either take time just holding her or him or provide a time for that child to enjoy a little privacy. I guess that would depend on the age. You could also introduce or remind him or her of encouraging verses you have found.

Journal

· Chapter 8 ·

TEN PERCENT OF WHAT?

> "There is no sin in possessing money. The sin comes when money begins to possess us."

Do you remember the awkward stage in life when you were too old to be in any kid class during Sunday morning church service, but too young to want to listen to what the pastor was saying? Perhaps you are forty-five and still don't want to hear what the pastor is saying. I eventually grew out of this stage, I think. I can remember, though, countless services (we went every time the doors were open, and there were so many services) where mom walked into the sanctuary with three kids who were, at times, challenging for any mom to handle. We were "the preacher's kids," and she probably felt a great need to keep us quiet.

Although I don't remember ever being obnox-iously wild, I do recall my mother's sharp whispers into my ear: "Do you want me to take you to the bathroom?" She would use her really hot breath as she spoke, and so I knew we would not be going there for any pleasant reason. Thus, I was forced to entertain myself quietly.

I would draw. I would play tic-tac-toe. I would trace my hand and decorate it. I would color my brother Chris' fingernails with a pencil and shade all the creases on his hand. I would push down the bulging blue-gray veins on the back of my mom's hand and then act grossed out that they would pop right back. (I used to think that was funny, but now that I have the same looking veins, it's not funny anymore.)

I used to try to sleep with my head on mom's lap, but unless you could put your legs up on the pew it wasn't very comfy. I would go through my mom's pictures. They were always the same, but I liked looking at them, anyway. I'd count how many she had of each family member to see if she loved us all equally.

On the rare occasion that my dad would be sitting with us, I loved sitting next to him. He would drape his big strong arm around my child-sized shoulders, and my head would rest back in his armpit with a perfect fit. As an adult, my dad's armpit would not be my first choice as a headrest, but at the time it was great. I actually look back with fondness to all these things and many more in which I learned to busy myself less and listen a little more.

There is one more thing, which happens to be the subject of this chapter, that I really enjoyed doing in the service. It began when I would hear, "Would the ushers please come forward." Immediately, I would ask Mom for some money to put in the offering plate. She'd get out her purse that always smelled like Chantilly perfume, rustle her hands along the bottom, and pull out a couple of coins. I would eagerly watch as the gold-plated dish was passed hand to hand my way. I loved to watch how much other people gave and wondered why some would give envelopes.

When the plate finally reached me, I'd drop my coins in one at a time so it would take longer. I was a little Pharisee, wasn't I? I also remember running my hands through the money as if I were going to pocket it just to get a "look" from my mother. It was fun putting money in that gold plate. Do you know why? Simple, it wasn't my money!

Now, as an adult, it's not quite as fun or exciting to put my money in that pretty gold plate as it passes by me on Sunday morning. Sometimes I am giving money away that I really feel I need, or at least really, really want. I have never had a high paying job, and in fact, most of my life I have never even had a job, at least not one that paid me a monetary paycheck. Even so, there are times I have made money that needed to be tithed, and so with the discipline of tithing, as with any discipline, there came more lessons in being prudent. Let's see how we can be more effective in this very important issue.

I'm fascinated by how much the Bible talks about money. Jesus used money in many of his illustrations. Let's look in the Book of Luke. In chapter 7 Jesus uses a story about monetary debt to help Simon better understand the tremendous gift of forgiveness. In chapter 12 Jesus warns us not to value our lives by the abundance of our possessions. In chapter 15 our Lord tells a familiar parable of a woman who loses one of her coins and the party she has when she finds it. He tells us this to try to give us a glimpse of the celebration in heaven over one sinner who repents.

Chapter 15 also tells about a boy who valued money so much he begged for his inheritance just to go out and blow it in the city. You know the story: once this boy is broke, he goes home only to find a very forgiving father. This father resembles our very forgiving heavenly Father who stretches his arms out to greet a broken son or daughter who had been lost spiritually but has been found. Jesus talks time and again about how the love of money can be cancerous to the spirit. "How hard it is for (a rich man) to enter the kingdom of God" (Luke 18:24). These are just a handful of the numerous illustrations about money. Why, this same book tells about Jesus being betrayed into the hands of killers by a man named Judas for a bag of coins (Luke 22:1–6). How sad it is to be lost in the lust of something as short-lived as money.

I'm bringing these scriptures to mind to point out a couple of common threads among the fabrics of men and women. We all have an understanding of money; some of us understand more than others. We all realize the fact that in this world money is a necessity. That is why, I believe, Jesus used money as an illustration so often—we can all identify with it.

There is no sin in possessing money. The sin comes when money begins to possess us. The other common thread, I believe, is that at the core of us all there is a selfish nature. How can we tell if money is possessing us? The one way I want to talk about is in the area of tithing. Do you find it odd that the God who "owns the cattle on a thousand hills" (Psalm 50:10) commanded his covenant people to give ten percent of all they gained? Is it because God needs it?

No, we don't tithe out of God's need; we tithe out of our need. To give, even such a small percent, serves as a thermometer to the health of our soul. If you feel such pain in giving ten percent back to the Lord that you are not able to do it, and with a good and willing spirit, you might need to look at who is in control of you. Look in the Scriptures at the blessings God gives to us if we would do something so simple as giving.

Malachi the prophet hears God speaking:

"Will a man rob God? Yet you rob me.
"But you ask, 'How do we rob you?'
"In tithes and offerings. You are under a curse— the whole nation of you—because you are robbing me. Bring the whole tithe into the storehouse, that there may be food in my house. Test me in this," says the Lord Almighty, "and see if I will not throw open the floodgates of heaven and pour out so much blessing that you will not have room enough for it. I will prevent pests from devouring your crops, and the vines in your fields will not cast their fruit," says the Lord Almighty. "Then all the nations will call you blessed, for yours will be a delightful land," says the Lord Almighty.
—Malachi 3:8–12

Isn't that incredible? I mean really incredible? If you just read that last paragraph and didn't get chills up your spine, go back and reread it. Continue reading it until you do respond, because it is a powerful scripture. "Test me in this," says the Lord Almighty, "and see if I will not throw open the floodgates of heaven and pour out so much blessing that you will not have room enough for it."

I think that's awesome. God has every right to ask us to give, but our God, our wonderful, generous God sees a giving heart and does what? He gives back in abundance! Now you may be saying, "Yeah, that's really great. But don't you realize that I can't tithe when I don't make any money."

There are many ways to tithe. Second Corinthians 8:12 beautifully says, "For if the willingness is there, the gift is acceptable according to what one has, not according to what he does not have." If you do not have a monetary offering to present to the Lord but there is a willingness to give within you, present yourself to the Lord. He knows you and your strengths. He knows where in your character there is plenty to share.

Ask God to bring some needs to your attention that will allow you to tithe out of the gifts in your character instead of your pocketbook. When a new person comes to church, invite that person to your home for a night of fellowship. God can use some of that gift of hospitality with which he blessed you. If you hear of a young single girl who has just had a baby, open your heart to her and teach her how to be a good mommy to her child by letting her observe you with your children. That would be tithing out of the vast storehouse of mothering wisdom that comes from experience. God has taught you a lot you could share.

Perhaps you can take a meal to a family who has just lost a loved one. I know from experience that when my family is in transition, not having to worry about what to make for dinner is a true blessing! Maybe you have an extra room in that house of yours. Call the church office and let them know that it is available to them if the need arises. It could be used to house a visiting pastor, a hurting teen, or even someone who is needing a time to get away and search for the Lord in quiet. Wow! There are so many different ways that you, prudent woman, can tithe out of the plentiful harvest in your character. God has done many good works in you. Give out of those areas in which God shows you have strength. In all the "tithing" you do be sure you do it with a sweet and gentle spirit, not begrudging the extra time it takes. The Lord loves a cheerful giver.

> Remember this: Whoever sows sparingly will also reap sparingly, and whoever sows generously will also reap generously. Each man should give what he has decided in his heart to give, not reluctantly or under compulsion, for God loves a cheerful giver.
>
> —2 Corinthians 9:6–7

EPILOGUE: SO IN CONCLUSION

> Do not store up for yourselves treasures on earth, where moth and rust destroy, and where thieves break in and steal. But store up for yourselves treasures in heaven, where moth and rust do not destroy, and where thieves do not break in and steal. For where your treasure is, there your heart will be also.
>
> —Matthew 6:19–21

All this talk about fixing up, painting, restoring, purchasing, and so forth, to improve our surroundings is entertaining and, I think, of some value; however, let us not put all our energy into things of this earth. Being prudent has some material benefits, but it can be much more useful when applied spiritually. To be prudent, once again, is to make sound judgments, not only about your money, but also about your time, your words, your actions, and your thoughts. A prudent woman is a woman of beauty, a woman who finds herself constantly taking inventory of her heart, her motives, and her values.

A PRAYER

Oh, Lord, make me prudent. Instill in me a desire to be responsible with each and every decision. Help me to come to you with all my needs and desires. Give me a new and a fresh understanding of you and how much you care for me. Help me as I deal with my children; I know these years are passing by me so quickly. How I live my life and the decisions I make affect them greatly. I am so thankful I can count on you and your perfect direction to help me.

Sometimes, Lord, I am not humble. Thank you for Jesus' example of true humility. I will try to follow His lead in humbleness with each person I meet.
Thank you, Lord, for all with which you have blessed me: my husband, my children, my friends and family, as well as my home. Thanks for each opportunity I get to fix our house up to match our own personalities. You are so great to meet all my

needs. Sometimes You do that through others. Please use me to prudently meet someone else's needs, too.

I love you, Lord! You are a wise, fun, awesome, and, yes, a prudent God! Amen.

May the Lord bless you as you go through your days. Best wishes for the changes you will make in your home as well as in your heart. I ask again, "Who wants to be the prudent woman?" I know I do, and I hope you do, too.

Journal

ON THE SURFACE ...

1. Do you tithe? (How's that for a basic question?)

_____

2. On a scale of "1" being depressed, and "10" being absolutely delighted, how cheerful are you when you tithe?

_____

_____

3. Would you rather tithe or eat that peanut butter ice cream with the big chunks of chocolate in it?

UNDER THE SKIN ...

1. What is it about money, do you think, that causes us such discomfort when it comes to giving it away?

_____

_____

_____

_____

2. In what area of your life do you feel God has blessed you so much you could tithe from it? Are you doing that right now?

_____

_____

_____

_____

NOW WHAT ...?

Write down five different ways you could tithe. Don't let any of them involve money. Put at least one of them into practice this week.

_____

_____

_____

_____

_____

SOMETHING TO PASS ON ...

Sit down with your child and talk about the different ways to tithe. If your child is at least over three he or she can participate in this. Ask him or her to think of something he or she can do to tithe out of God's blessings to them.

Journal

PUTTING IT ALL TOGETHER ...

ON THE SURFACE

1. What would you consider to be the most "prudent" decision or action you have done in the last week?

_____

_____

_____

_____

2. What is a synonym for "prudent"?

_____

Journal

UNDER THE SKIN ...

Let me repeat the verse we read early on, "Houses and wealth are inherited from parents, but a prudent wife is from the LORD" (Proverbs 19:14). "A prudent wife is from the Lord!" Isn't that great! A woman who strives to be faithful to her God in her decisions, attitudes, and so forth is nothing short of a gift.—A gift from God Almighty to your man (or your future man). Well, tie a big bow on my head and call Paul because his little gift is here! You know God doesn't just go to Kmart and pick up a pack of prudent ladies. He has to teach, build, repair, remodel, and recycle us into the women he has destined us to be. The outcome is gift-worthy. I hope by reading this book you have felt God's hands challenging you to do a little remodeling in your own life. Let's talk about those now.

1. List three areas in which you feel God is calling you to be more prudent:

    a) _____

    b) _____

    c) _____

2. Write a prayer giving these to the Lord.

_____

_____

_____

_____

NOW WHAT ...?

I suggest writing out some goals of how you would like to become a more prudent woman and sharing those with a friend. Ask this friend to hold you accountable to these goals. (Isn't *accountable* a scary word?)

SOMETHING TO PASS ON ...

Teach your children the disciplines of being prudent focusing on the three things you wrote down. For instance if you wrote down, "I feel God is wanting me to cut up my VISA (He is telling me that—I cut it up but I saved the number—I can still shop by phone) then you can really be a great example to your child by not impulse shopping.

Once Adam went to Kindergarten and came home announcing I had forgotten to send him lunch money. I gasped and said, "Oh no, Adam, What did you do?" He said with an experienced shoppers attitude, "I told the lady, Charge it!" At that point it started to dawn on me I might not be passing on a prudent legacy in this particular area. How much more healthy is it for our children to see their mom really wanting an item but having to wait on it for a while! These computer keys are hurting my heart with every push because this is not an area I am comfortable surrendering. How about you? Decide on different areas of prudent growth you can share with your children. God will bless you for it. Being prudent is the gift that keeps on giving.

Journal

Journal

Journal

Journal

Journal